asian grilling

THE ESSENTIAL KITCHEN

asian grilling

VICKI LILEY

PERIPLUS

contents

Beef, Pork and Lamb 76

Beef and mint rolls • Barbecued rack of lamb • Grilled beef with tomato and fresh chili relish • Pork and apple skewers • Korean style steak • Soy beef skewers • Whole beef tenderloin with papaya relish • Chinese style pork tenderloin • Grilled steak with chili pepper and basil butter

Vegetables and Fruit 94

Tofu and scallion satays • Spicy eggplant dip with fried wontons • Potato and rosemary skewers • Grilled vegetables with warm ginger dressing • Grilled pears with warm rice pudding • Grilled mango and peaches with raspberry coulis

asian grilling

Grilling is one of the oldest and simplest forms of cooking, and it is an inexpensive means of cooking a vast variety of foods.

Grilling food has been a way of life for decades throughout Asia, and street food is a mainstay in many southeast Asian countries. Snacks of satay chicken, stir-fried noodles, dumplings and pancakes are enjoyed on street corners, under temple canopies, cotton umbrellas, silk awnings and widespread green trees. It's a brilliant kaleidoscope of noise and vividly contrasting smells. The tastes are intense, hot, sweet, salty and bitter. At many street markets, locals also display an array of locally grown fruit and vegetables along with brightly colored crafts and clothing, all for barter or sale.

This enjoyable alfresco style of eating demands the freshest ingredients and, because these street foods frequently have to be displayed, cooked and sold without refrigeration, the turnover must be rapid and the heat of the cooking intense. The spicing and marinating often contribute to preserving the foods as well as adding flavor.

Asian Grilling reflects the flavors and cooking traditions of many Asian countries, including Singapore, Vietnam, Thailand, China and Korea.

There are many varieties of barbecues and pans available. Outdoor and indoor grilling is essentially the same, but outdoor barbecues lend themselves to garden entertaining areas where friends and family can gather while the meal is cooking. Indoor grilling can be done on a tabletop with a Japanese-style hibachi or electric countertop grill, or in a stove-top grill pan in the kitchen—all small by scale to an outdoor barbecue, but still a fast, unique way of cooking with friends and family.

The choice of a barbecue or a grill pan will depend on several things, including the number of people you will entertain, the location of the barbecue, storage and the size of the cooking area needed. For example, if the cooking area is too small, the grill will become congested and food won't cook properly. If it's too large, you will waste fuel. Do you want a barbecue that lights automatically, or do you want the challenge of starting a fire? Select a model and type that suits your needs.

Asian-style grilling generally requires only a small grill or barbecue. The Japanese-style hibachi is ideal for Asian-style grilling. Compact, portable, and inexpensive, it is suitable for small balconies and for either indoor or outdoor cooking. It uses charcoal for its heat source.

The modern electric countertop grill has a nonstick surface, generally has three or more heat settings and can be opened flat for a larger cooking surface.

Chargrill pans are available in cast iron or nonstick aluminum and are used on gas or electric stove tops. They are easy to clean and store and are ideal for everyday cooking for up to six people. A well-ventilated kitchen or exhaust hood is recommended for this style of indoor cooking.

RIDGED GRILL PAN

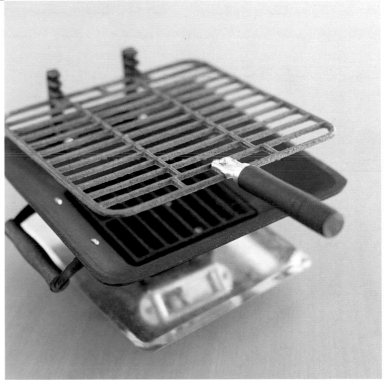

HIBACHI GRILL

The easy-to-use barbecue has multiple heat settings and is available in many sizes and models in all price ranges. Some are connected to a home's gas supply, while others use portable gas bottles or tanks. Kettle grills, heated by charcoal, are available in various lidded sizes, small up to very large. The smaller models are ideal for Asian grilling.

Disposable barbecues, which use presoaked charcoal briquettes, are inexpensive and require no messy clean up. They must be used on a heatproof rock or brick base and disposed of carefully, once completely cold.

Light-weight portable barbecues, generally heated with charcoal or wood chips, are simply a smaller version of the home barbecue and are ideal for Asian grilling anywhere.

Getting started

Starting a gas grill is easy. Open the lid and make sure that the burner controls are off and that there is fuel in the tank or bottle. Turn on the fuel and light the barbecue according to the manufacturer's instructions. Allow the grill to preheat on high for 10 minutes before cooking.

If using charcoal grills, charcoal briquettes make a good fire and are easy to use. The most common way to start a charcoal fire is to build a pyramid of charcoal on a grate in the fire pan, soak it with the lighter fluid if the briquettes aren't presoaked and light it carefully. Be sure to purchase good quality briquettes, as many of the cheaper brands can impart a chemical flavor to food.

A popular and ecological alternative to using lighter fluid or presoaked briquettes is the charcoal chimney starter, a sheet metal cylinder, available at barbecue outlets. Place the chimney starter on the barbecue grate, stuff crumpled newspaper in the base, pile charcoal briquettes on top and light the paper. Either way, the coals are ready when they are covered with pale grey ash, generally in about 20 minutes. Carefully distribute the coals from the pyramid or tip them from the chimney starter onto the barbecue grate.

You are now ready to start grilling.

For electric countertop grills, plug into the power source, turn on and preheat according to the manufacturer's instructions. For stove-top chargrill pans, place the clean pan over high heat on the stove and preheat for 5 minutes before cooking. For disposable barbecues, follow the manufacturer's instructions.

Equipment

Long-handled utensils, like tongs, fork and metal spatula, are essential for turning foods during cooking. Keep a separate pair of long-handled tongs for moving coals around if need be. Heatproof mitts are also essential for a successful barbecue, and basting brushes and an apron may come in handy.

Controlling the heat

Heat is regulated in a charcoal grill by moving the briquettes with a set of long-handled tongs. Push them closer together to intensify the heat, or spread them apart to cool the fire down. The air vents on the barbecue provide a similar control. Open them to increase the heat level, or close them down to decrease it. On a gas barbecue, the control dials make it easy to maintain the heat source to suit your cooking. If flames flare up on a gas barbecue, don't spray with water. The steam can cause burns and can sometimes crack the enamel finish on your barbecue. Instead, close the lid and close the air vents.

Cleaning

Follow manufacturer's instructions for cleaning gas, charcoal and other barbecues. To clean the cooking grill of a gas barbecue, turn the burners to high, close the lid and allow to heat for 5 minutes. Then use a long-handled wire brush to scrape off any food residue. When the grill cools, remove it and clean with hot soapy water. Keep the bottom tray and grease-catch pan clean to prevent fires.

Skewers

Grilled food on skewers has an attractive appeal to cooks and diners alike because of the different flavors, textures and colors that can be cooked and served as one unit. Threading combinations of food onto skewers can also make small quantities of expensive ingredients go a long way.

The foods threaded onto skewers should have the same cooking time, or longer cooking foods such as potato should be parboiled beforehand. Bamboo skewers need soaking in water for 10 minutes before any food is threaded onto them to prevent them from burning.

Both bamboo and stainless steel skewers are available in many sizes. Select the size best suited for the food and the occasion. For example, small cubes of chicken for a party are best threaded onto small bamboo skewers so guests can dispose of the skewers after eating. Stainless steel skewers require cleaning after each use.

Fresh rosemary and bay leaf stems can be used as an attractive and flavorsome alternative to bamboo or stainless steel skewers. However, make sure the stems are woody, not the young soft stems, and soak them in water before use. Lemongrass, sugarcane and bamboo shoots are also sometimes used as skewers for food.

Marinating

One of the easiest ways to add flavor to food before grilling is to marinate it. Foods can be marinated for a few minutes or up to several hours, and even overnight. The longer the marinating time, the stronger the flavor will be, so don't marinate delicately flavored foods like fish for too long. Marinating also enhances the moisture level of the food, keeping it juicy and more succulent after cooking. Leftover marinades can be brushed over the food whilst it is cooking, or heated and served as a sauce with the cooked meal, but make sure always to boil the marinade for one minute before serving.

Select a mix of ingredients that compliment the food to be marinated. For example, cilantro (fresh coriander) and lime juice compliment the subtle flavor of fish and seafood. Strong marinades may sometimes overpower the food itself.

Because many marinades have an acid-based ingredient like citrus juice or wine, it is best to marinate food in a shallow nonmetallic dish.

Heavy-duty plastic storage bags are also great for marinating foods.

Prepared marinades can be stored in screw-top jars in the refrigerator for up to two weeks.

Quick-and-easy marinades

Place any of the following marinade ingredients into a screw-top jar, shake to mix, then brush over food. Cover and refrigerate the food for 10 minutes or more, then drain and grill.

Fish, seafood and chicken (1 lb/500 g each)

2 tablespoons vegetable oil

2 tablespoons Thai sweet chili sauce

2 tablespoons lemon or lime juice

3 cloves garlic, chopped

3 teaspoons grated ginger

1 tablespoon chopped cilantro (fresh coriander) leaves

salt and pepper to taste

Beef, lamb and pork (1 lb/500 g each)

2 tablespoons vegetable oil

1 tablespoon chopped basil leaves

3 tablespoons soy sauce

grated rind of 1 lemon

3 cloves garlic, chopped

salt and pepper to taste

Vegetables (1 lb/500 g)

2 tablespoons vegetable oil

2 teaspoons sesame oil

2 cloves garlic, chopped

2 teaspoons grated ginger

salt and pepper to taste

Fruit

2 tablespoons lemon or lime juice

1 tablespoon honey

1 teaspoon grated ginger

Step-by-step marinating

1 Prepare marinade ingredients; mix well.

2 Place fish, chicken, meat or vegetables into a shallow nonmetallic dish.

3 Brush or pour marinade over food. Cover and refrigerate for 10 minutes (for a light marinade) or longer.

4 Drain, then cook on preheated grill or barbecue to desired doneness.

Dry coatings

Dry mixtures of breadcrumbs, herbs and spices can add flavor and texture to food to be grilled. They can also protect the food from the harsh heat of the grill, resulting in a more subtle, grilled flavor. A simple coating of breadcrumbs can keep food moist inside while creating a crisp and crunchy outside. A blend of spices rubbed into the food's surface before cooking can add flavor and enhance the food's natural taste. Food coated in a blend of fresh herbs and spices can be left to marinate for several hours before cooking.

Dry coatings are best suited to thinner portions of foods that will cook quickly so the coatings don't burn. Partially cook longer cooking foods before coating and grilling them.

Easy dry coatings

Brush food to be grilled with oil and coat in one of the following mixtures.

Fish and seafood (for 2 fish fillets)

grated rind of 1 lemon or 1 lime

2 tablespoons chopped cilantro (fresh coriander) leaves

1 tablespoon chopped chervil

sea salt and freshly ground black pepper to taste

Chicken (for 4 chicken breast fillets)

3 tablespoons fresh white breadcrumbs

1 small red chili pepper, seeds removed and chopped

2 tablespoons chopped basil leaves

grated rind of 1 lime

1 clove garlic, finely chopped

sea salt and freshly ground black pepper to taste

Beef, lamb and pork (1 lb/500 g each)

1 teaspoon five spice powder

1 teaspoon sea salt

1 teaspoon freshly ground black pepper

2 tablespoons chopped cilantro (fresh coriander) leaves

1 small red chili pepper, seeded and chopped

Step-by-step coatings

1 Prepare ingredients..

2 Brush fish, chicken, seafood, or meat with oil.

3 Coat food in prepared coating mixture.

4 Cook on a preheated, oiled grill or barbecue to desired doneness.

Flavored butters

A slice of flavored butter placed onto a hot-from-the-grill piece of fish, chicken, meat or vegetable forms a warm buttery sauce. Flavored butters are a quick and tasty means of adding additional seasonings. Butters can be made up to 3–4 days ahead of time or frozen for up to 2 months. Flavored butters are rolled into logs, then sliced, scooped or piped onto cooked foods. They are also a delicious spread for warm grilled bread.

Basic flavored butter recipes
In a bowl, mix all ingredients until well combined.

Fish and seafood (1 lb/500 g)

OPTION 1:

4 oz (125 g) softened butter

grated rind and juice of 1 lime

OPTION 2:

4 oz (125 g) softened butter

2 tablespoons chopped cilantro (fresh coriander) leaves

1 tablespoon chopped chervil

1 clove garlic, chopped

juice of 1 lemon

Beef, lamb and pork (1 lb/500 g each)

Option 1:

4 oz (125 g) softened butter

2 teaspoons chopped rosemary

1 small red chili pepper, seeded and finely chopped

freshly ground black pepper

OPTION 2:

4 oz (125 g) softened butter

2 cloves garlic, chopped

2 scallions (shallots/spring onions), finely chopped

freshly ground black pepper

Chicken (1 lb/500 g)

OPTION 1:

4 oz (125 g) softened butter

2 canned anchovy fillets, drained and mashed

juice of 1 lemon

freshly ground black pepper

OPTION 2:

4 oz (125 g) softened butter

2 cloves garlic, finely chopped

1 small green chili pepper, seeded and finely chopped

grated rind and juice of 1 lime

Step-by-step flavored butters

1 Using a wooden spoon or an electric mixer, beat butter until soft.

2 Add flavorings and mix well.

3 Spoon onto a piece of plastic wrap and shape into a log. Roll up and chill until firm.

4 Slice into rounds to serve.

ingredients

When purchasing fresh ingredients such as garlic chives, kaffir lime leaves, lemongrass, mizuna, chili peppers, red (Spanish) onion, Thai basil and Vietnamese mint, purchase only the amount you need as they will not stay fresh for a long time in the refrigerator. Grains and spices can be stored in the pantry. Chili oil and hoisin sauce should be stored in the refrigerator after opening (hoisin sauce can be stored indefinitely).

ARBORIO RICE

BUCKWHEAT NOODLES

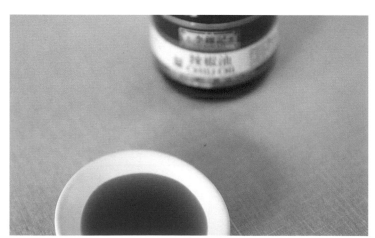

CHILI OIL

FIVE SPICE

FRESH GINGER

GARLIC CHIVES

HOISIN SAUCE

KAFFIR LIME LEAVES

LEMONGRASS

MIZUNA

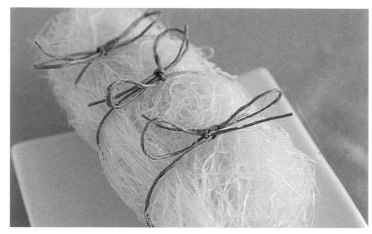

RICE VERMICELLI NOODLES

RED CHILI PEPPERS

RED (SPANISH) ONION

RICE NOODLES

STAR ANISE

THAI BASIL

VIETNAMESE MINT

WASABI

WONTON WRAPPERS

Grilled coconut chicken

1¹/₄ cups (10 fl oz/300 ml) thin coconut cream or
  coconut milk

3 cloves garlic, finely chopped

2 small red chili peppers, seeded and finely chopped

1 teaspoon freshly grated ginger

¹/₂ cup (1 oz/30 g) fresh cilantro (coriander) leaves

grated rind and juice of 1 lime

3 tablespoons soy sauce

1 tablespoon fish sauce

1 tablespoon grated palm sugar or brown sugar

4 chicken breast fillets, with skin

1 tablespoon vegetable oil

1 bunch (13 oz/400 g) bok choy, rinsed and cut in
  half lengthwise

For marinade, place coconut cream, garlic, chili peppers, ginger, cilantro, rind, juice, soy sauce, fish sauce and sugar into a food processor or blender. Process until smooth, about 30 seconds.

Place chicken fillets onto a cutting board, make 3 slits in skin side of each fillet using a sharp knife. Place chicken into a shallow nonmetallic dish. Pour marinade ingredients over chicken and cover dish with plastic wrap. Refrigerate for 2 hours. Drain chicken, reserving marinade.

Preheat a grill pan or barbecue, then brush grill lightly with oil. Grill chicken until tender, 4–5 minutes each side. Test chicken by piercing the thickest part with a skewer; chicken is cooked if the juices run clear. Remove from grill.

Meanwhile, steam or blanch bok choy in a saucepan of boiling water until tender crisp, about 2 minutes. Place reserved marinade ingredients into a small saucepan. Stir over medium heat and bring to a boil. Boil for one minute, remove from heat and set aside. To serve, arrange bok choy on serving plates and top each with a chicken fillet. Drizzle with warm marinade. Serve any extra marinade in a separate serving dish.

Serves 4

GRILLED COCONUT CHICKEN

Grilled chicken and Asian greens salad

$^1/_2$ oz (15 g) rice vermicelli noodles

2 small thin eggplants (aubergines), thinly sliced lengthwise into $^1/_{16}$-inch (2-mm) slices

4 chicken breast fillets

2 tablespoons vegetable oil

2 cloves garlic, finely chopped

2 cups (2 oz/60 g) mixed Asian salad leaves (mizuna, tah soi, watercress, snow pea shoots)

$^1/_4$ cup (1 oz/30 g) fresh bean sprouts, rinsed

8 cherry tomatoes, quartered

$^1/_2$ red (Spanish) onion, cut into very thin wedges

FOR DRESSING

2 teaspoons sesame oil

1 tablespoon vegetable oil

3 teaspoons freshly grated ginger

$^1/_4$ cup (2 fl oz/60 ml) fresh lime juice

2 tablespoons mirina

Place noodles into a heatproof bowl and cover with boiling water. Allow to stand until softened, about 10 minutes; drain. Using scissors, snip noodles into shorter lengths.

Brush eggplant and chicken fillets with combined oil and garlic. Preheat a grill pan or barbecue and grill eggplant slices until golden and tender, about 1 minute each side. Remove and cut each slice in half. Grill chicken fillets until golden and tender, about 4–5 minutes each side. Test chicken by piercing the thickest part with a skewer; chicken is cooked if the juices run clear. Remove from grill and allow to stand 5 minutes before slicing each into 8 diagonal slices. Arrange chicken on serving plates.

Combine noodles, eggplant, salad leaves, bean sprouts, tomatoes and onion. Toss until well combined. Divide among serving plates. Drizzle with dressing and serve immediately.

To make dressing: Combine oils, ginger, lime juice and mirin in a screw-top jar. Shake well to mix.

Serves 4

GRILLED CHICKEN AND ASIAN GREENS SALAD

Spicy chicken skewers with mint yogurt

1 lb (500 g) chicken breast fillets

3 teaspoons ground coriander

2 teaspoons ground turmeric

1 small red chili pepper, seeded and
   finely chopped

4 cloves garlic, finely chopped

2 tablespoons superfine (caster) sugar

1 teaspoon sea salt

12 bamboo skewers

2 tablespoons peanut oil

6½ oz (200 g) choy sum or other Asian greens,
   roughly chopped

MINT YOGURT

½ cup (4 fl oz/125 ml) plain (natural) yogurt

2 cloves garlic, finely chopped

2 tablespoons freshly chopped mint leaves

¼ cup (1½ oz/40 g) peeled, seeded and
   chopped cucumber

Cut chicken fillets into 1½-inch (4-cm) cubes. Combine ground coriander, turmeric, chili pepper, garlic, sugar and salt. In a bowl, toss chicken pieces in spice mixture. Cover bowl with plastic wrap and refrigerate for 2 hours. Soak bamboo skewers in water for 10 minutes, then drain. Thread chicken pieces onto bamboo skewers. Preheat a grill pan or barbecue, then brush grill with oil. Grill chicken skewers until golden and tender, 2–3 minutes each side.

Steam or blanch choy sum in boiling water for 3 minutes or until tender crisp, then drain. Serve chicken warm with mint yogurt and steamed choy sum.

To make mint yogurt: Combine yogurt, garlic, mint and cucumber. Mix until well combined. Cover and chill before serving.

Serves 4

SPICY CHICKEN SKEWERS WITH MINT YOGURT

Chili chicken and cilantro pizzettas

FOR PESTO

³/₄ cup (1 oz/30 g) well packed basil leaves

¹/₄ cup (¹/₃ oz/10 g) well packed fresh cilantro
  (coriander) leaves

3 cloves garlic

2 oz (60 g) pine nuts

2 oz (60 g) freshly grated parmesan cheese

¹/₃ cup (3 fl oz/90 ml) virgin olive oil

FOR CHICKEN TOPPING

2 chicken breast fillets, with skin

4 tablespoons vegetable oil

4 cloves garlic, finely chopped

2 small red chili peppers, seeded and finely chopped

FOR PIZZETTAS

4 tablespoons tomato paste

2 cloves garlic, finely chopped

2 teaspoons chili oil

2 ready-made pizza bases, 12-inches (30-cm) each

¹/₂ oz (15 g) baby arugula (rocket) leaves, rinsed

To make pesto: Place basil and cilantro in a food processor and process until finely chopped, about 30 seconds. Add garlic, pine nuts and cheese and process until finely ground, about 30 seconds. With food processor running, gradually add olive oil and process until the mixture becomes a thick paste, about 1 minute.

To make chicken: Using a sharp knife, pierce the skin side of each chicken fillet 3–5 times, and place chicken in a shallow nonmetallic dish. In a bowl, combine 2 tablespoons vegetable oil, garlic and chili peppers and pour over chicken fillets. Cover dish with plastic wrap and refrigerate for 1 hour; drain. Preheat a grill pan or barbecue, then brush grill with the remaining oil. Grill chicken fillets until golden and tender, 4–5 minutes each side. Test chicken by piercing the thickest part with a skewer; chicken is cooked if the juices run clear. Remove from grill and allow to stand 5 minutes before thinly slicing diagonally.

To make pizzettas: Preheat oven to 350°F (180°C/Gas 4). In a bowl, combine tomato paste, garlic and chili oil; mix well. Remove pizza bases from packaging and cut into 4-inch (10-cm) rounds using a cookie (biscuit) cutter and spread each with a little tomato paste mix. Place onto a baking tray lined with parchment (baking paper). Bake at 350°F (180°C/Gas 4) until crisp, 12–15 minutes. Remove from oven and top each with a spoonful of pesto, arugula leaves and slices of chicken fillet. Serve warm as a snack or with drinks.

Makes 12

Hint

Leftover pesto, topped with a thin covering of oil, can be stored in a screw-top jar in the refrigerator for 3–4 days.

CHILI CHICKEN AND CILANTRO PIZZETTAS

Five spice grilled chicken

2 young chickens (spatchcocks), about

  1 lb (16 oz/500 g) each

1 teaspoon sesame oil

1 tablespoon rice wine

4 tablespoons peanut oil

1 teaspoon five spice powder

1 teaspoon grated ginger

1 clove garlic, finely chopped

1 tablespoon honey

2 tablespoons soy sauce

1 bunch choy sum, about 16 oz (500 g)

1 red (Spanish) onion, cut into 8 wedges

Clean chickens and pat dry with paper towel. Using poultry shears, cut chickens in half through the backbones and breastbones and place them in a shallow nonmetallic dish. Combine sesame oil, rice wine, 2 tablespoons of peanut oil, five spice powder, ginger, garlic, honey and soy and mix until well combined. Brush mixture over chicken skin, then cover dish with plastic wrap and refrigerate for 3 hours. Drain chicken, reserving marinade.

Preheat a barbecue, then lightly brush grill with the remaining peanut oil. Grill chicken halves on barbecue until golden and tender, about 8 minutes each side, brushing with reserved marinade during cooking. Test chicken by piercing the thickest part with a skewer; chicken is cooked if the juices run clear. Remove from barbecue. Grill onion wedges until lightly browned, 1–2 minutes. Steam or blanch choy sum in boiling water until tender-crisp, about 2 minutes; drain. To serve, place choy sum onto serving plates, top with a chicken half, and garnish with red onion wedges.

Serves 4

Hint

This recipe is best suited to an outdoor barbecue. However, if only an indoor grill pan is available, grill chicken halves until golden, then bake in a 350°F (180°C/Gas 4) oven for 10–15 minutes to cook through. Otherwise substitute chicken halves for chicken breast fillets.

FIVE SPICE GRILLED CHICKEN

Star anise chicken fillet with ginger risotto

4 chicken breast fillets, with skin

4 tablespoons vegetable oil

1 tablespoon rice wine

1 tablespoon soy sauce

1 tablespoon honey

2 tablespoons freshly grated ginger

2 cloves garlic, finely chopped

2 whole star anise

FOR GINGER RISOTTO

5 1/2 cups (44 fl oz/1.35 L) chicken stock

2 whole star anise

3 tablespoons olive oil

1 onion, chopped

1 clove garlic, finely chopped

2 teaspoons freshly grated ginger

1 1/2 cups (10 1/2 oz/330g) arborio rice

1/4 cup (1/3 oz/10 g) chopped fresh cilantro
   (coriander) leaves

sea salt and freshly ground black pepper to taste

To make chicken: Using a sharp knife, pierce the skin side of each chicken fillet 3–5 times. Place chicken in a shallow nonmetallic dish. In a bowl, combine 2 tablespoons oil, rice wine, soy sauce, honey, ginger, garlic and star anise and pour over chicken fillets. Cover dish with plastic wrap and refrigerate for 3 hours. Drain chicken, reserving marinade.

Preheat a grill pan or barbecue, then lightly brush grill with the remaining oil. Grill chicken fillets until golden and tender, 4–5 minutes each side, brushing with reserved marinade during cooking. Test chicken by piercing the thickest part with a skewer; chicken is cooked if the juices run clear. Remove from grill.

To make risotto: Place stock and star anise into a medium-sized saucepan and bring to a boil over high heat. Reduce heat to low and allow stock to simmer. Warm oil in a medium-large saucepan over medium heat. Add onion, garlic and ginger and cook, stirring, until onion softens, about 2 minutes. Add rice, cook for 1 minute, stirring constantly until rice is coated with oil. Add 1 cup stock to the pan, stirring constantly. Reduce heat, and allow to simmer gently while stirring. Gradually add the remaining stock 1 cup at a time until the rice is al dente and creamy. Stir in cilantro and season with salt and pepper.

To serve, spoon ginger risotto onto serving plates and top with chicken. Serve warm.

Serves 4

Spicy grilled chicken kibbeh

24 small bamboo skewers

2 oz (60 g) fine burghul (cracked wheat)

12 oz (375 g) chicken thigh fillets,
coarsely chopped

$^1/_2$ teaspoon ground all spice

$^1/_4$ teaspoon ground cayenne pepper

1 teaspoon ground cumin

$^1/_2$ teaspoon sea salt

$^1/_2$ teaspoon freshly ground black pepper

$^1/_2$ onion, roughly chopped

$^1/_2$ cup ($^3/_4$ oz/20 g) well packed mint leaves,
finely chopped

2 tablespoons vegetable oil

FOR DIPPING SAUCE

2 tablespoons olive oil

$^1/_4$ cup (2 fl oz/60 ml) lemon juice

$^1/_2$ teaspoon cracked black pepper

lemon wedges, for serving

Soak bamboo skewers in water for 10 minutes, then drain. Place burghul into a bowl and cover with cold water. Allow to stand 10 minutes then drain. Squeeze out excess liquid using your hands. Place chicken, all spice, cayenne pepper, cumin, salt, pepper and onion in a food processor and process until finely minced, about 30 seconds. Transfer mixture to a bowl, add burghul and mint, and mix until well combined. Divide into 24 portions. Shape each into a log shape and insert a skewer into each. Preheat a grill pan or barbecue, then lightly brush grill with oil. Grill skewers until kibbeh is golden and tender, about 3–4 minutes. Remove from grill and serve warm with dipping sauce and lemon wedges.

To make dipping sauce: Combine oil, lemon juice and pepper and chill before serving.

Serves 6

SPICY GRILLED CHICKEN KIBBEH

Barbecue soy chicken

4 young chickens (spatchcocks), 1 lb (500 g) each

1/3 cup (3 fl oz/90 ml) soy sauce

1 teaspoon sugar

3 tablespoons mirin

4 tablespoons olive oil

1 tablespoon grated ginger

2 cups (2 oz/60 g) salad greens such as watercress
  and snowpea shoots, for serving

Clean chickens and pat dry with paper towel. Truss chicken wings and legs securely with wetted string and place chickens in a shallow nonmetallic dish. Combine soy sauce, sugar, mirin, 2 tablespoons olive oil and ginger and brush over chicken skin. Cover dish with plastic wrap and refrigerate for 1 hour. Drain, reserving marinade. Preheat a barbecue, then brush lightly with the remaining oil. Grill chickens until golden and tender, 15–20 minutes, brushing with reserved marinade and turning chickens during cooking. Test chicken by piercing the thickest part with a skewer; chicken is cooked if the juices run clear. Remove from heat and serve hot or cold with salad greens.

Serves 4

Hint

This recipe is best suited to an outdoor barbecue.

BARBECUE SOY CHICKEN

Lime chicken and pork patties

1 lb (500 g) ground (minced) chicken thigh meat

8 oz (250 g) ground (minced) lean pork meat

8 scallions (shallots/spring onions), chopped

3 cloves garlic, finely chopped

3 small red chili peppers, one seeded and finely chopped, 2 seeded and sliced

1/4 cup (1/3 oz/10 g) finely chopped fresh cilantro (coriander) leaves

2 teaspoons grated kaffir lime rind

2 tablespoons kaffir lime juice

1 1/2 cups (3 oz/90 g) fresh white breadcrumbs

1 egg, beaten

2 tablespoons vegetable oil

12 fresh basil leaves

1 baby Romaine (cos) lettuce, leaves separated and washed, for serving

Place chicken, pork, scallions, garlic, chopped chili pepper, cilantro, rind, juice, breadcrumbs and egg in a large mixing bowl. Using wet hands, mix until well combined. Divide into 12 portions and shape each into a round patty. Place in a single layer on a plate, cover with plastic wrap and refrigerate for 1 hour.

Preheat a grill pan or barbecue, then brush grill lightly with oil. Grill patties until golden and tender, 2–3 minutes each side. Remove from grill. Warm leftover vegetable oil in a small saucepan and fry basil leaves and the 2 sliced chili peppers until aromatic, about 1 minute.

To serve, place chicken patties onto servings plates with lettuce leaves and top each with fried basil and chili peppers.

Serves 4

Grilled chicken fillet with eggplant

4 chicken breast fillets

4 scallions (shallots/spring onions),
 roughly chopped

4 cloves garlic

1 tablespoon chopped basil leaves

1 tablespoon chopped fresh cilantro
 (coriander) leaves

$^1/_3$ cup (3 fl oz/90 ml) soy sauce

1 teaspoon five spice powder

2 tablespoons mirin

1 tablespoon fish sauce

1 teaspoon sesame oil

1 tablespoon rice wine

2 teaspoons sugar

2 tablespoons vegetable oil

6 small thin eggplants (aubergines), sliced
 lengthwise into $^1/_{16}$-inch (2-mm) slices

2 cups (2 oz/60 g) mizuna leaves, rinsed

Place the chicken in a shallow nonmetallic dish. Place scallions, garlic, basil, cilantro, soy sauce, five spice powder, mirin, fish sauce, sesame oil, rice wine and sugar into a food processor and process until well blended, about 30 seconds. Pour marinade over chicken fillets, cover dish with plastic wrap and refrigerate for 2 hours. Drain chicken, reserving marinade. Preheat a grill pan or barbecue, then brush grill lightly with vegetable oil. Grill chicken fillets until golden and tender, 4–5 minutes each side, brushing with reserved marinade during cooking. Test chicken by piercing the thickest part with a skewer; chicken is cooked if the juices run clear. Remove from grill. Lightly brush eggplant slices with oil and grill until golden and tender, 1–2 minutes each side. Place reserved marinade into a small saucepan and stir over medium heat and bring to a boil; allow to boil for 1 minute, then set aside. To serve, arrange mizuna leaves on serving plates, top with eggplant then a chicken fillet. Drizzle with warm marinade.

Serves 4

GRILLED CHICKEN FILLET WITH EGGPLANT

seafood

Grilled polenta cakes with stir-fried shrimp

FOR POLENTA CAKES

8 oz (250 g) instant polenta (cornmeal)

$^1/_3$ cup ($^1/_3$ oz/15–20 g) finely chopped basil leaves

3 cloves garlic, finely chopped

$^1/_4$ cup (1 oz/30 g) freshly grated parmesan cheese

$^1/_4$ cup (2 oz/60 g) butter

2 tablespoons olive oil

FOR STIR-FRIED SHRIMP

2 tablespoons vegetable oil

3 cloves garlic, crushed

1 small red chili pepper, seeded and chopped

2 lb (1 kg) jumbo shrimp (king prawns) peeled and
  deveined, leaving tails intact

4 vine ripened tomatoes, stems removed and
  chopped

1 cup (1 oz/30 g) loosely packed basil leaves

To make polenta cakes: Cook polenta as directed on packet. Remove from heat and stir in basil, garlic, parmesan and butter, mixing until butter melts. Spoon polenta into an oiled 8-inch by 10-inch (20-cm by 25-cm) shallow pan and smooth surface with a spatula. Set aside and allow to cool for 1 hour. Turn out polenta onto a cutting board and cut into 6 rectangles. Brush both sides of polenta pieces with olive oil. Preheat a grill pan or barbecue and grill polenta cakes until golden, 2–3 minutes each side. Remove from grill. Serve warm with stir-fried shrimp.

To stir-fry shrimp: Warm oil in a wok or frying pan. Add garlic and chili pepper and stir-fry over medium heat until aromatic, about 1 minute. Add shrimp and stir-fry until shrimp change color, 4–5 minutes. Add tomato and stir-fry for 2 minutes. Remove from heat, add basil leaves and toss through. Serve immediately.

Serves 6

Lime and chili pepper sardines with green aioli

36 fresh sardines, cleaned, heads removed
   and butterflied
2 tablespoons vegetable oil
1 teaspoon grated lime rind
1 tablespoon lime juice
1 small red chili pepper, seeded and
   finely chopped
1 tablespoon chopped fresh cilantro
   (coriander) leaves
1/4 teaspoon sea salt
1/4 teaspoon freshly ground black pepper
1 1/2 cups (1 1/2 oz/45 g) mizuna

FOR GREEN AIOLI
6 scallions (shallots/spring onions),
   roughly chopped
1/4 cup (1/3 oz/10 g) chopped basil leaves
3 cloves garlic, chopped
3 egg yolks
2 tablespoons lemon juice
3/4 cup (6 fl oz/180 ml) virgin olive oil
sea salt and freshly ground black pepper

Pat sardines dry with paper towel and place in a shallow nonmetallic dish. Combine 2 tablespoons oil, rind, juice, chili pepper, cilantro, salt and pepper and mix well. Brush over sardines and let stand for 5 minutes. Preheat a grill pan or barbecue, then brush grill with the remaining oil. Grill sardines for 1–2 minutes each side. Remove from grill. To serve, arrange mizuna on serving plates and top with warm sardines. Serve with green aioli.

To make green aioli: Place scallions, basil, garlic, egg yolks and lemon juice into a food processor. Process until smooth, about 30 seconds. Gradually add olive oil while food processor motor is running and process until the mixture becomes a thick sauce. Add salt and pepper to taste.

Serves 6

Hint

Leftover aioli can be stored in a screw-top jar in the refrigerator.

LIME AND CHILI PEPPER SARDINES WITH GREEN AIOLI

Thai grilled seafood curry

12 jumbo shrimp (king prawns), peeled and
   deveined, leaving tails intact

12 oz (375 g) swordfish, cut into 2¹/₂-inch
   (6-cm) chunks

16 scallops, cleaned

¹/₄ cup (2 fl oz/60 ml) peanut oil

6¹/₂ oz (200 g) baby green beans

3–4 teaspoons ready-made Thai green curry paste
   (to taste)

2 teaspoons additional peanut oil

2 cloves garlic, finely chopped

1¹/₂ cups (12 fl oz/375 ml) thin coconut cream or
   coconut milk

3 kaffir lime leaves, crushed

3 teaspoons fish sauce

2 teaspoons soy sauce

1 teaspoon shaved palm sugar or brown sugar

1 tablespoon chopped basil leaves

1 tablespoon chopped fresh cilantro
   (coriander) leaves

Pat seafood dry with paper towel and brush with oil. Preheat a grill pan or barbecue. Working in batches, grill shrimp until shrimp change color, 2–3 minutes, then remove from heat. Grill scallops until the opaque flesh turns white, 2–3 minutes, then remove from heat. Grill fish pieces until flesh is firm, 2–3 minutes, then remove from heat.

Blanch green beans in a saucepan of boiling water for 2 minutes, then drain. Combine beans and seafood, cover and keep warm.

Place curry paste, 2 teaspoons of oil and garlic into a wok or saucepan. Stir over medium heat until aromatic, about 2 minutes. Stir in thin coconut cream, lime leaves, fish sauce, soy sauce and sugar. Reduce heat to low and simmer for 10 minutes. Do not allow to boil. Remove from heat and stir in basil and cilantro. Divide seafood and beans among serving bowls and spoon curry sauce over each bowl. Serve with steamed jasmine rice.

Serves 4

THAI GRILLED SEAFOOD CURRY

Spicy marinated tuna

4 fresh tuna steaks (approximately 6 oz/180 g each)

2 tablespoons soy sauce

$1/_3$ cup (3 fl oz/80 ml) mirin

1 tablespoon sesame oil

1 teaspoon cracked black pepper

1 teaspoon ground cumin

1 teaspoon five spice powder

1 teaspoon sugar

1 teaspoon sea salt

$1^1/_2$ cups ($1^1/_2$ oz/45 g) mizuna

lime wedges, for serving

Place tuna into a shallow nonmetallic dish. In a bowl, combine soy sauce, mirin and sesame oil and brush over tuna. Cover dish with plastic wrap and refrigerate for 30 minutes. Drain, reserving marinade. Combine pepper, cumin, five spice powder, sugar and salt and mix well. Sprinkle spice mix over tuna steaks. Preheat a grill pan or barbecue. Grill tuna, allowing it to remain pink in the center, 3–4 minutes each side. Remove from grill and allow to stand for 3 minutes. Pour reserved marinade into a small saucepan and bring to a boil over medium heat; boil for 1 minute, then set aside. Cut each tuna steak into wedges, arrange on serving plates and drizzle with warm marinade. Serve with mizuna and lime wedges.

Serves 4

SPICY MARINATED TUNA

Fresh salmon cakes

1 lb (500 g) boneless and skinless salmon fillets

2 tablespoons vegetable oil

2 lb (1 kg) potatoes, peeled and chopped

3 tablespoons chopped dill

2 small red chili peppers, seeded and chopped

3 teaspoons freshly grated ginger

grated rind of 1 lime

1 teaspoon sea salt

$^1/_2$ teaspoon freshly ground pepper

$^1/_2$ cup (2$^1/_2$ oz/75 g) plain flour

2 eggs, beaten

2 tablespoons milk

3 cups (6 oz/180 g) fresh white breadcrumbs

Preheat a grill pan or barbecue, then brush grill with 1 tablespoon oil. Grill salmon until fish flakes easily when tested with a fork, 3–4 minutes each side (salmon should be cooked completely through). Remove from grill and allow to cool. Place potatoes into a saucepan of boiling water and cook until tender, about 8 minutes, then drain and mash. Allow to cool 10 minutes. Add salmon, dill, chili peppers, ginger, rind, salt and pepper. Using wet hands, mix thoroughly. Cover with plastic wrap and refrigerate for 1 hour. Divide into 12 portions and shape them into patties. Coat each patty in flour, dip into combined egg and milk, then coat in breadcrumbs.

Preheat a grill pan or barbecue and carefully brush grill with remaining oil. Cook salmon cakes until golden, 2–3 minutes each side. Remove from grill and serve warm or chilled with green aioli (see page 44 for recipe).

Serves 4

FRESH SALMON CAKES

Grilled shrimp salad

24 jumbo shrimp (king prawns) peeled and
   deveined, leaving tails intact

2 tablespoons peanut oil

$^3/_4$ oz (25 g) cellophane noodles

$^1/_2$ green papaya, skinned and cut into
   matchstick lengths

1 mango, skinned and cut into matchstick lengths

1 cup (1 oz/30 g) loosely packed fresh cilantro
   (coriander) leaves

$^1/_2$ cup ($^1/_2$ oz/15 g) loosely packed fresh
   basil leaves

$^1/_4$ cup ($^3/_4$ oz/25 g) sliced scallions
   (shallots/spring onions)

FOR DRESSING

1 small red chili pepper, seeded and
   finely chopped

3 tablespoons fish sauce

4 tablespoons lime juice

1 teaspoon sesame oil

2 teaspoons grated ginger

1 teaspoon shaved palm sugar or brown sugar

Brush shrimp with oil. Preheat a grill pan or barbecue and grill shrimp until they change color, 3–4 minutes, turning during cooking. Remove from grill. Place noodles in a heatproof bowl, pour in boiling water to cover and allow to stand until noodles soften, about 10 minutes. Drain and, using scissors, roughly cut noodles into shorter lengths.

Combine noodles, shrimp, papaya, mango, cilantro, basil and scallions in a mixing bowl. Add dressing and toss until well combined. Serve at room temperature or chilled.

To make dressing: Place chili pepper, fish sauce, lime juice, sesame oil, ginger and sugar in a screw-top jar. Shake well to mix.

Serves 4

GRILLED SHRIMP SALAD

Garlic and chili pepper scallops

1 lb (500 g) scallops

3 cloves garlic, finely chopped

$1/2$ teaspoon five spice powder

1 teaspoon grated ginger

1 small red chili pepper, seeded and finely chopped

2 tablespoons soy sauce

1 tablespoon rice wine

2 tablespoons vegetable oil

3 tablespoons water

1 cup (1 oz/30 g) mizuna

Place scallops in a shallow nonmetallic dish. In a bowl, combine garlic, five spice powder, ginger, chili pepper, soy sauce and rice wine, and pour over scallops. Cover dish with plastic wrap and refrigerate for 30 minutes. Drain scallops, reserving marinade. Preheat a grill pan or barbecue, then brush grill with oil. Grill scallops until the opaque flesh turns white, 2–3 minutes, turning during cooking. Remove from grill.

Place reserved marinade into a saucepan. Add water, bring to a boil and allow to boil for 1 minute; set aside. To serve, arrange mizuna on serving plates. Top with scallops and drizzle with warm marinade.

Serves 2–3

Mixed seafood skewers

12 bamboo skewers

8 oz (250 g) jumbo shrimp (king prawns) peeled and deveined, leaving tails intact

8 oz (250 g) scallops, cleaned

12 oz (375 g) white fish fillets, cut into 1½-inch (4-cm) cubes

4 tablespoons peanut oil, divided in half

½ onion, roughly chopped

2 cloves garlic

2 teaspoons grated ginger

2 stems lemongrass (white section only), chopped

1 teaspoon shrimp paste

4 tablespoons soy sauce

1 teaspoon chili oil

1 teaspoon sesame oil

1 cup (1 oz/30 g) mizuna

Soak bamboo skewers in cold water for 10 minutes, drain. Pat shrimp, scallops and fish dry with paper towel and thread alternately onto skewers. Brush seafood skewers with 2 tablespoons peanut oil, then place into a shallow nonmetallic dish.

Place onion, garlic, ginger, lemongrass, shrimp paste, the remaining oil, 1 tablespoon soy sauce, chili oil and sesame oil into a food processor and process until mixture becomes a smooth paste, about 30 seconds. Brush seafood with spice paste, then cover dish with plastic wrap and refrigerate for 30 minutes.

Preheat a grill pan or barbecue. Grill seafood skewers until seafood changes color, 3–4 minutes each side. Remove from grill. Serve warm with remaining soy sauce as a dipping sauce and fresh mizuna.

Serves 4

MIXED SEAFOOD SKEWERS

Chili pepper, salt and pepper calamari

2 small red chili peppers, seeded and
  finely chopped

1 tablespoon sea salt

1 teaspoon cracked black pepper

2 tablespoons vegetable oil

16 baby squid (calamari), about 2 lb (1 kg),
  cleaned and halved

1¹/₂ cups (1¹/₂ oz/45 g) mizuna

Combine chili pepper, salt and pepper. Brush squid pieces with oil and press chili pepper mix into both sides of squid. Preheat a grill pan or barbecue. Grill squid pieces for 15–30 seconds each side. Remove from grill and serve on a bed of mizuna.

Serves 2–4

CHILI PEPPER, SALT AND PEPPER CALAMARI

Grilled salmon with wasabi butter

1/2 cup (4 oz/125 g) butter, softened

2 teaspoons wasabi paste

grated rind of 1 lime

1 tablespoon lime juice

1/2 teaspoon freshly ground black pepper

2 tablespoons vegetable oil

4 salmon fillets (approximately 6 1/2 oz/180 g each), skin and bones removed

fresh cilantro (coriander) leaves, for garnish

FOR CRISPY FRIED POTATOES

3 potatoes, peeled and very thinly sliced

1/2 cup (4 fl oz/125 ml) vegetable oil, for frying

Place butter in a mixing bowl and beat until soft. Add wasabi, rind, juice and pepper and mix until well combined. Refrigerate until firm. Brush salmon with oil. Preheat a grill pan or barbecue. Grill salmon 2–3 minutes each side (salmon should remain pink in the center), then allow to stand 5 minutes before cutting in half. Place onto serving plates. Using a teaspoon or melon baller, scoop wasabi butter onto fish. Serve with crispy fried potatoes and garnish with fresh cilantro.

To make crispy fried potatoes: Pat potatoes dry with paper towel. Heat oil over medium heat and, working in batches, fry potato slices until golden and crisp, about 2 minutes. Remove with a slotted spoon and drain on paper towel.

Serves 4

Hint

Leftover wasabi butter can be stored in a sealed container in the refrigerator for up to 2 weeks.

GRILLED SALMON WITH WASABI BUTTER

Tuna and egg with rosemary

4 tuna steaks (approximately 6^1/$_2$ oz/200 g each)

8 small stems fresh rosemary

string

2 tablespoons vegetable oil

4 eggs

GARLIC BUTTER SAUCE

^{1}/$_4$ cup (2 oz/60 g) butter

3 cloves garlic, finely chopped

1 small red chili pepper, seeded and
  finely chopped

1 tablespoon chopped fresh cilantro
  (coriander) leaves

^{1}/$_4$ teaspoon sea salt

^{1}/$_4$ teaspoon freshly ground black pepper

Place tuna steaks onto a cutting board and top each with 2 stems of fresh rosemary. Secure rosemary with string, tying like a parcel. Preheat a grill pan or barbecue, then brush grill with oil. Grill tuna 2 minutes each side (tuna should remain pink on the inside). Remove from grill and keep warm. Poach eggs in a saucepan of simmering salted water for 3–4 minutes. Remove with a slotted spoon and drain. To serve, place tuna onto serving plates, top each with a poached egg, then drizzle with garlic butter sauce.

To make garlic butter sauce: Place butter, garlic and chili pepper into a small saucepan. Stir over medium heat until butter melts. Cook until butter bubbles, about 1 minute. Remove from heat and stir in cilantro, salt and pepper. Serve immediately over tuna and egg.

Serves 4

TUNA AND EGG WITH ROSEMARY

Barbecued shrimp

1½ lb (750 g) jumbo shrimp (king prawns)

⅓ cup (3 fl oz/90 ml) vegetable oil

3 teaspoons sesame oil

1 tablespoon chopped fresh cilantro
 (coriander) leaves

3 kaffir lime leaves, finely shredded

3 cloves garlic, finely chopped

1 tablespoon rice wine

lemon or lime wedges, for serving

Remove heads from shrimp. Pull out and remove veins (a bamboo skewer is good for this), leaving shell intact. Place shrimp in a shallow nonmetallic dish. Combine oils, cilantro, lime leaves, garlic and rice wine; mix well and pour over shrimp. Cover with plastic wrap and refrigerate overnight. Remove shrimp from marinade. Preheat a grill pan or barbecue. Grill shrimp until shrimp change color, 2–3 minutes each side. Remove from grill and allow to cool 5 minutes before serving with fresh lemon or lime wedges.

Serves 4

Hint

Place a bowl of cold water with a slice of lemon on the table and plenty of paper napkins alongside so guests can rinse their hands after peeling shrimp.

BARBECUED SHRIMP

Salmon with cilantro crust

4 tablespoons chopped fresh cilantro
   (coriander) leaves

1 tablespoon grated lime rind

2 teaspoons freshly ground black pepper

1 teaspoon sea salt

2 tablespoons chopped chervil

pinch dried chili flakes

1 clove garlic, finely chopped

4 tablespoons vegetable oil, divided in half

4 salmon fillets (approximately 6½ oz/
   200 g each), bones and skin removed

FOR GARLIC MASH

4 potatoes, peeled and chopped

1 tablespoon olive oil

3 cloves garlic, finely chopped

½ teaspoon sea salt

In a bowl, combine cilantro, rind, pepper, salt, chervil, chili flakes and garlic and mix until well combined. Brush salmon with 2 tablespoons oil, then lightly coat both sides of each salmon fillet with herb mixture. Preheat a grill pan or barbecue, then brush grill with the remaining oil. Grill salmon 2–3 minutes each side (salmon should remain pink on the inside). Remove from grill and allow to stand 3 minutes before slicing in half. Serve warm with garlic mash.

To make garlic mash: Cook potatoes in a saucepan of boiling salted water until tender, about 8 minutes. Drain and mash. Add olive oil, garlic and salt, and mix until well combined.

Serves 4

SALMON WITH CILANTRO CRUST

Shrimp, lime and chili pepper skewers

12 bamboo skewers

12 jumbo shrimp (king prawns) peeled, deveined, leaving tails intact

4 tablespoons vegetable oil

3 tablespoons lime juice

2 teaspoons grated ginger

2 cloves garlic, finely chopped

2 limes, cut into 6 wedges each

12 small red chili peppers

2 red (Spanish) onions, cut into 6 wedges each

1 1/2 cups (1 1/2 oz/45 g) mixed salad greens, for serving

Soak bamboo skewers in cold water for 10 minutes, then drain. Place shrimp in a shallow nonmetallic dish. Combine 2 tablespoons oil, juice, ginger and garlic, mix well and pour over shrimp. Cover dish with plastic wrap, and refrigerate for 1 hour. Remove shrimp from marinade. Thread a shrimp, lime wedge, chili pepper and red onion wedge onto each skewer. Preheat a grill pan or barbecue, then brush grill with the remaining oil. Grill skewers until shrimp change color, 2–3 minutes each side. Remove from grill and serve warm with salad greens.

Serves 3–4

Sesame tuna

1 egg white

1 tablespoon soy sauce

4 tuna steaks, approximately 6$\frac{1}{2}$ oz (200 g) each

$\frac{1}{3}$ cup (1 oz/30 g) sesame seeds

2 tablespoons vegetable oil

1 tablespoon sesame oil

4 oz (125 g) rice stick noodles

lemon wedges, for serving

In a bowl, lightly beat egg white with a fork and add soy sauce. Brush one side of each tuna steak with egg white mixture, then dip egg white side of tuna into sesame seeds. Preheat a grill pan or barbecue, then brush grill with vegetable oil. Grill tuna, sesame seed side down first, for 2–3 minutes each side (tuna should remain pink on the inside). Remove from grill and allow to stand 5 minutes before slicing in half. Warm sesame oil in a small saucepan over medium heat for 1 minute. To serve, place tuna onto a serving plate and drizzle with warm sesame oil. Serve with rice noodles and a wedge of fresh lemon.

To make rice stick noodles: Place noodles in a heatproof bowl and cover with boiling water. Allow to soften for 15 minutes, then drain. Or cook in a saucepan of boiling water for 3 minutes, then drain. Serve noodles on the plate with tuna.

Serves 4

SESAME TUNA

Fish cutlet with sake

4 fish steaks (cutlets), approximately 6¹/₂ oz
(200 g) each (choose any fish with firm, white
flesh, such as sea bass, grouper, halibut, coley
or blue-eye cod)

2 teaspoons sea salt

1 teaspoon freshly ground black pepper

2 tablespoons vegetable oil

1 fl oz (30 ml) sake

juice and grated rind of 1 lime

2 cups (2 oz/60 g) baby spinach leaves,
for serving

2 tablespoons additional grated lime rind

Sprinkle both sides of fish with salt and pepper. Preheat a grill pan or barbecue, then brush grill with oil. Grill fish until fish changes color and flakes easily with a fork, 2–3 minutes each side. Remove from grill and brush each with combined sake, juice and rind. To serve, arrange spinach leaves on serving plates and top with fish cutlets. Serve with extra lime rind.

Serves 4

FISH CUTLET WITH SAKE

Fish bites with coconut sambal

12 oz (375 g) firm white boneless, skinless fish fillets

1½ teaspoons ground turmeric

1 teaspoon sea salt

2 teaspoons cornstarch (cornflour)

¼ teaspoon ground chili powder

2 tablespoons vegetable oil

2 cups (10 oz/300 g) steamed jasmine rice

2 tablespoons chopped fresh cilantro
  (coriander) leaves

garlic chives, for garnish

COCONUT SAMBAL

⅓ cup (1½ oz/45 g) unsweetened shredded
  (desiccated) coconut

3 tablespoons boiling water

½ teaspoon shrimp paste

1 kaffir lime leaf, finely shredded

¼ onion, finely chopped

2 teaspoons lemon juice

Cut fish into ¾-inch by 2½-inch (2-cm by 6-cm) lengths. In a bowl, combine turmeric, salt, cornstarch and chili powder, mix well and rub spice mixture into fish pieces. Preheat a grill pan or barbecue, then brush grill with oil. Grill fish pieces until fish is firm, 1–2 minutes each side. Remove from grill. Combine cooked rice with cilantro. Serve fish bites with rice and coconut sambal. Garnish with garlic chives.

To make coconut sambal: Place coconut in a heatproof bowl, pour in boiling water and mix well. Add shrimp paste, curry leaves, onion and lemon juice. Cover and refrigerate until serving.

Serves 4

FISH BITES WITH COCONUT SAMBAL

lamb

Beef and mint rolls

12 oz (375 g) tenderloin or sirloin (rump or fillet)
  steak

3 cloves garlic, finely chopped

2 teaspoons fish sauce

1 teaspoon sesame oil

2 tablespoons vegetable oil

FOR ROLLS

1 English (hothouse) cucumber, cut into matchstick
  lengths 2½ inches by ¼ inch (6 cm by ½ cm)

3 scallions (shallots/spring onions), green
  section only

12 round rice paper wrappers, 6-inch (15-cm)
  in diameter

36 large mint leaves

3 fl oz (90 ml) soy sauce, for serving

Place steak in a shallow nonmetallic dish. In a bowl, combine garlic, fish sauce and sesame oil, mix well and brush over meat. Cover dish with plastic wrap and refrigerate for 30 minutes. Remove meat from marinade.

Preheat a grill pan or barbecue, then brush grill with vegetable oil. Grill steak until tender, 3–4 minutes each side (beef should remain pink in the center). Remove from grill, cover with aluminum foil and allow to stand for 5 minutes. Using a very sharp knife, slice steak very thinly.

To prepare rolls: Dip scallions into a bowl of boiling water until softened, about 15 seconds, then remove and refresh in a bowl of ice water. Cut each scallion in 4 lengthwise.

Half fill a bowl with warm water, and place a paper towel onto your work surface. Dip a rice paper wrapper into the warm water until soft, about 15 seconds, then place onto a clean paper towel. Place 3 mint leaves and 3 cucumber lengths into the center of the wrapper, top with a small amount of sliced beef and roll up into a cylinder. Tie a scallion length around each roll, then snip off both ends of roll using scissors. Repeat with remaining ingredients, covering prepared rolls with a damp towel to prevent them drying out. Serve with soy sauce as a dipping sauce.

Serves 3–4

BEEF AND MINT ROLLS

Barbecued rack of lamb

3 fl oz (90 ml) lime juice

3 fl oz (90 ml) olive oil

3 tablespoons chopped fresh cilantro
   (coriander) leaves

5 cloves garlic, finely chopped

2 teaspoons sea salt

1 teaspoon freshly ground black pepper

3 teaspoons ground cumin

1 teaspoon ground coriander

2 racks of lamb, 8 cutlets each, excess fat trimmed

2 tablespoons additional olive oil

4 limes, cut in half

3 tablespoons chili jam, for serving

In a bowl, combine juice, olive oil, cilantro, garlic, salt, pepper, cumin and coriander and mix until well combined. Place lamb in a shallow nonmetallic dish and brush with herb mixture. Cover dish with plastic wrap and refrigerate for 3–4 hours. Remove lamb from marinade.

Preheat a grill pan or barbecue, then brush grill with 2 tablespoons oil. Grill lamb until just pink in the center when cut, about 8 minutes each side. Remove from heat, cover with aluminum foil and allow to stand for 5 minutes. Barbecue lime halves until lightly golden, 1–2 minutes. Slice lamb racks into 2 cutlet sections and serve warm with lime and chili jam.

Serves 6–8

Hint

This recipe is best suited to an outdoor barbecue.

BARBECUED RACK OF LAMB

Grilled beef with tomato and fresh chili relish

1 lb (500 g) sirloin or porterhouse
  (rump or sirloin) steak

1 teaspoon sesame oil

3 tablespoons vegetable oil

3 cloves garlic, chopped

$^1/_4$ cup ($^1/_2$ oz/15 g) fresh cilantro (coriander) leaves

$^1/_4$ cup ($^1/_3$ oz/10 g) chopped basil leaves

1 cup (1 oz/30 g) fresh watercress, for serving

FOR TOMATO AND FRESH CHILI RELISH

1 small ripe tomato, finely chopped

1 small red chili pepper, seeded and finely chopped

$^1/_4$ red (Spanish) onion, finely chopped

2 kaffir limes leaves, finely shredded

3 tablespoons fish sauce

2 tablespoons lime juice

2 teaspoons shaved palm sugar or brown sugar

Remove any excess fat from meat and place in a shallow nonmetallic dish. Place sesame oil, 1 tablespoon vegetable oil, garlic, cilantro and basil into a food processor and process until the mixture becomes a thick paste, about 30 seconds. Spread paste over both sides of meat. Cover dish with plastic wrap and refrigerate for 1 hour.

Preheat a grill pan or barbecue, then brush grill with remaining oil. Grill steak, 2–3 minutes per side (or longer if you prefer well done). Remove from grill, cover with aluminum foil and allow to stand for 5 minutes. Using a sharp knife, slice steak thinly and serve with tomato and fresh chili relish, garnished with fresh watercress.

To make tomato and fresh chili relish: Combine tomato, chili pepper, onion, lime leaves, fish sauce, juice and sugar and mix well. Cover and refrigerate until serving.

Serves 2–4

GRILLED BEEF WITH TOMATO AND FRESH CHILI RELISH

Pork and apple skewers

24 bamboo skewers

1 lb (500 g) pork tenderloin (fillets), cut into
   1½-inch (4-cm) cubes

2 red apples, cut into 12 wedges each

5 tablespoons vegetable oil

2 tablespoons lime juice

1 tablespoon soy sauce

2 tablespoons chopped fresh cilantro
   (coriander) leaves

2 kaffir lime leaves, finely shredded

1 tablespoon Thai basil

1 teaspoon sea salt

1 teaspoon freshly ground black pepper

1 clove garlic, finely chopped

Soak skewers in cold water for 10 minutes, then drain. Place pork and apple wedges onto skewers and place in a shallow nonmetallic dish. In a bowl, combine 3 tablespoons oil, juice, soy sauce, cilantro, lime leaves, basil, salt, pepper and garlic and mix well. Brush over pork and apple, cover dish with plastic wrap and refrigerate for 30 minutes. Drain off marinade.

Preheat a grill pan or barbecue, then brush grill with remaining oil. Grill skewers until pork is tender, 2–3 minutes per side. Remove from grill and serve warm.

Serves 6–8

PORK AND APPLE SKEWERS

Korean style steak

1 lb (500 g) tenderloin (scotch fillet) steak

3 tablespoons soy sauce

1 tablespoon sugar

3 cloves garlic, finely chopped

2 teaspoons grated ginger

3 teaspoons sesame oil

3 tablespoons vegetable oil

2 tablespoons toasted sesame seeds

1 nashi pear, cut into 12 very thin slices

2 scallions (shallots/spring onions)

1/2 head iceberg lettuce, cut into 4 wedges

Place steak in a freezer bag and freeze for 1 hour. Remove from freezer, slice very thinly and place in a nonmetallic dish. In a bowl, combine soy sauce, sugar, garlic, ginger, sesame oil, 1 tablespoon vegetable oil and 1 tablespoon sesame seeds, and mix well. Pour over meat and mix until well combined. Cover dish with plastic wrap and refrigerate for 30 minutes. Drain off marinade.

Preheat a grill pan or barbecue, then brush grill with remaining oil. Grill meat for 30 seconds each side. Remove from grill. Grill pear wedges until lightly golden, about 30 seconds. Cut scallions into thin 2½-inch (6-cm) long strips and place into a bowl of iced water until scallions curl, about 5 minutes; drain. Serve sliced beef with grilled pear and a wedge of lettuce. Garnish with scallion curls and remaining sesame seeds.

Serves 4

KOREAN STYLE STEAK

Soy beef skewers

12 bamboo skewers

8 oz (250 g) sirloin (rump) steak

5 tablespoons soy sauce

2 tablespoons oyster sauce

1 teaspoon sugar

2 tablespoons mirin

2 teaspoons sesame oil

1 clove garlic, finely chopped

1 tablespoon chopped fresh cilantro
   (coriander) leaves

2 tablespoons vegetable oil

Soak skewers in cold water for 10 minutes, then drain. Slice steak into thin long strips, about 1 inch by 4 inches (2.5 cm by 10 cm). Thread strips onto skewers and place in a shallow nonmetallic dish. In a bowl, combine 2 tablespoons soy sauce, oyster sauce, sugar, mirin, sesame oil, garlic and coriander, and mix well. Brush marinade over beef, cover with plastic wrap and refrigerate for 30 minutes. Drain off marinade.

Preheat a grill pan or barbecue, then brush grill with oil. Grill beef skewers until tender, 2–3 minutes. Remove from grill and serve hot with remaining soy sauce as a dipping sauce.

Serves 3–4

SOY BEEF SKEWERS

Whole beef tenderloin with papaya relish

1½ lb (750 g) piece whole beef tenderloin (fillet)

2 teaspoons chili oil

3 tablespoons chopped basil leaves

2 tablespoons chopped fresh cilantro
   (coriander) leaves

4 tablespoons vegetable oil

6 thin slices prosciutto (Italian ham)

FOR PAPAYA RELISH

½ small fresh papaya, skin removed, seeded
   and chopped

4 shallots, sliced

2 tablespoons chopped basil leaves

2 tablespoons chopped fresh cilantro
   (coriander) leaves

3 fl oz (90 ml) Thai sweet chili sauce

Truss beef with string to hold in shape and place in a shallow nonmetallic dish. In a bowl, combine chili oil, basil, cilantro and 2 tablespoons vegetable oil and mix well. Spread mixture over meat, cover dish with plastic wrap and refrigerate for 1 hour.

Meanwhile, grill or pan-fry prosciutto until golden and crisp. Remove and drain on paper towel. Allow to cool, then break each in half and set aside.

Preheat a barbecue, then brush grill with remaining vegetable oil. Grill beef for 12–15 minutes, turning during cooking. Remove from grill, wrap in aluminum foil and allow to stand for 10 minutes, then cut into 4 thick steaks. To serve, place crisp prosciutto pieces onto serving plates, top with beef steak and spoon papaya relish over beef. Serve immediately.

To make papaya relish: Combine papaya, shallots, basil leaves, cilantro and chili sauce, and mix well. Refrigerate until serving.

Serves 4–6

WHOLE BEEF TENDERLOIN WITH PAPAYA RELISH

Chinese style pork tenderloin

1 lb (500 g) pork tenderloin (fillet)

3 tablespoons soy sauce

1 tablespoon hot bean paste

2 tablespoons hoisin sauce

4 cloves garlic, finely chopped

$^{1}/_{4}$ teaspoon five spice powder

1 tablespoon shaved palm sugar or brown sugar

2 tablespoons vegetable oil

$^{1}/_{4}$ Chinese cabbage, shredded

Place pork in a shallow nonmetallic dish. In a bowl, combine soy, hot bean and hoisin sauces, garlic, five spice and sugar and mix well. Pour mixture over pork, cover dish with plastic wrap and refrigerate for 2–3 hours. Drain pork, reserving marinade.

Preheat a grill pan or barbecue, then brush grill with vegetable oil. Grill pork until tender, 4–5 minutes each side, brushing with reserved marinade during cooking. Remove from grill, wrap in aluminum foil and allow to stand for 5 minutes.

Cook cabbage in a saucepan of boiling water until tender, 3–5 minutes. Drain and spoon into serving bowls. Thickly slice pork and serve on top of warm cabbage.

Serves 4

CHINESE STYLE PORK TENDERLOIN

Grilled steak with chili pepper and basil butter

4 oz (125 g) butter, softened

2 tablespoons chopped fresh cilantro
 (coriander) leaves

2 tablespoons chopped basil leaves

2 teaspoons grated lime rind

1 small red chili pepper, seeded and chopped

$^{1}/_{2}$ teaspoon freshly ground black pepper

$6^{1}/_{2}$ oz (200 g) dried buckwheat noodles

4 tenderloin (scotch fillet or fillet) steaks, about
 $6^{1}/_{2}$ oz (200 g) each

1 tablespoon olive oil

5 teaspoons chili oil

Place butter into a mixing bowl and beat until soft. Add cilantro, basil, rind, chili pepper and pepper and mix until well combined. Spoon onto a piece of plastic wrap, roll into a log shape and refrigerate until firm, about 15 minutes.

Cook buckwheat noodles in a saucepan of boiling water until tender, 5–6 minutes; drain.

Brush steaks with combined olive oil and 1 teaspoon chili oil. Preheat a grill pan or barbecue. Grill steaks until cooked to your liking, 2–3 minutes each side. Remove from grill and place onto serving plates.

Slice butter into $^{1}/_{4}$-inch (6-mm) rounds and place onto hot steaks. Serve with buckwheat noodles and remaining chili oil for dipping.

Serves 4

Tofu and scallion satays

12 bamboo skewers

12 oz (375 g) firm tofu, cut into 1¼-inch
   (3-cm) cubes

8 scallions (shallots/spring onions) cut into
   2-inch (5-cm) lengths

2 tablespoons soy sauce

1 teaspoon sesame oil

1 clove garlic, finely chopped

2 tablespoons vegetable oil

FOR SATAY SAUCE

3 tablespoons smooth peanut butter

4 cloves garlic, chopped

1 teaspoon chili oil

2 tablespoons soy sauce

pinch sea salt

2 teaspoons sugar

2 tablespoons hot water

1 tablespoon hot bean paste

Soak skewers in cold water for 10 minutes, then drain. Place tofu and scallion lengths alternately onto bamboo skewers and place skewers in a shallow dish. In a bowl, combine soy sauce, sesame oil and garlic and brush over tofu and scallions. Cover dish with plastic wrap and refrigerate for 30 minutes. Drain off marinade.

Preheat a grill pan or barbecue, then cook tofu and scallion skewers until golden, 1–2 minutes each side. Remove from grill and serve warm with satay sauce.

To make satay sauce: Place peanut butter, garlic, chili oil, soy sauce, salt, sugar, hot water and hot bean paste into a food processor. Process until smooth.

Serves 3–4

Hint

Leftover satay sauce can be stored in a screw-top jar in the refrigerator for up to 7 days.

TOFU AND SCALLION SATAYS

Spicy eggplant dip with fried wontons

2 medium eggplants (aubergines), thinly sliced

2 tablespoons olive oil

3 cloves garlic, chopped

$^1/_2$ cup ($^2/_3$ oz/20 g) chopped fresh cilantro
  (coriander) leaves

juice of 3 lemons

$^1/_2$ teaspoon sea salt or to taste

$^1/_2$ teaspoon freshly ground black pepper

$^1/_2$ cup (4 fl oz/125 ml) tahini

FOR FRIED WONTON WRAPPERS

24 fl oz (750 ml) vegetable oil, for deep frying

36 wonton wrappers

Brush eggplant slices with olive oil. Preheat a grill pan or barbecue. Grill eggplant slices until slightly blackened on both sides, 1–2 minutes each side. Remove from grill and allow to cool. Place eggplant, garlic, cilantro, lemon juice, salt, pepper and tahini into a food processor and process to a thick paste. Spoon into serving bowls and refrigerate before serving with fried wonton wrappers.

To make fried wonton wrappers: Heat oil in a large, deep heavy-based saucepan or deep fryer until it reaches 375°F (190°C) on a deep frying thermometer or until a small cube of bread dropped in oil sizzles and turns golden. Working with 2–3 wonton wrappers at a time, deep fry until golden, 1–2 minutes. Using a slotted spoon, remove from oil and drain on paper towels.

Serves 6–8

Potato and rosemary skewers

12 long woody stems of fresh rosemary

1 1/2 lb (750 g) sweet potatoes

12 small baby potatoes (chats)

2 tablespoons vegetable oil

1 teaspoon chili oil

1 teaspoon dried thyme leaves

2 cloves garlic, finely chopped

1/4 teaspoon freshly ground black pepper

1 teaspoon sea salt

1/3 cup (3 fl oz/90 ml) Thai sweet chili sauce,
   for dipping

Trim rosemary stems to 6 inches (15 cm) long and remove the leaves 4 inches (10 cm) from base of stem. Soak stems in cold water for 30 minutes, then drain.

Peel sweet potatoes and cut into 4 cm cubes. Cook sweet potato cubes and baby potatoes in a large saucepan of salted water until tender when pierced with a skewer, 8–10 minutes. Drain and refresh under cold running water. Pat vegetables dry with paper towel and cut each baby potato in half.

Thread potatoes carefully onto rosemary stems and place in a shallow dish. In a bowl, combine oils, thyme leaves, garlic, salt and pepper and brush over potatoes. Cover dish with plastic wrap and stand for 30 minutes. Preheat a grill pan or barbecue, then grill potato and rosemary skewers until golden, 1–2 minutes each side. Remove from grill and serve hot with Thai sweet chili sauce as a dipping sauce.

Serves 3–4

Grilled vegetables with warm ginger dressing

2 baby fennel, cut in half lengthwise

4 baby bok choy, cut in half lengthwise

4 small eggplants (aubergines), cut in half lengthwise

2 red (Spanish) onions, cut into 6 wedges each

2 long red chili peppers, cut in half lengthwise

12 fresh asparagus spears, trimmed

2 tablespoons vegetable oil

3 cloves garlic, finely chopped

FOR WARM GINGER DRESSING

3 teaspoons sesame oil

2 tablespoons vegetable oil

3 teaspoons freshly grated ginger

1/3 cup (3 fl oz/90 ml) fresh lime juice

2 tablespoons mirin

Place prepared vegetables in a shallow dish. In a bowl, combine oil and garlic and toss through vegetables until well coated.

Preheat a grill pan or barbecue. Working in batches, grill vegetables until golden, 1–2 minutes each side. Remove from grill, place into serving bowls and drizzle with warm ginger dressing. Serve immediately.

To make warm ginger dressing: Place oils, ginger, lime juice and mirin into a small saucepan. Whisk over a low heat until just warm, about 1 minute, and serve.

Serves 2–4

Grilled pears with warm rice pudding

FOR WARM RICE PUDDING

1 cup (7 oz/220 g) short grain rice

40 fl oz (1.25 L) milk

1 vanilla bean

1/2 cup (3 1/2 oz/105 g) superfine (caster) sugar

3/4 cup (6 fl oz/180 ml) cream

FOR GRILLED PEARS

4 firm pears, halved

juice of 1 lemon

1 tablespoon honey

2 tablespoons vegetable oil

To make warm rice pudding: Preheat oven to 300°F (150°C/Gas 2). Place rice in a medium-sized heatproof bowl. Cover rice with boiling water, allow to stand 3 for minutes, then drain. Place rice into a medium-sized, heavy-based saucepan. Add milk, vanilla bean and sugar. Stir over a low heat for 35 minutes. Remove vanilla bean and stir in cream. Transfer to a greased medium-sized heatproof dish and bake in preheated oven until rice is tender, about 30 minutes.

To grill pears: Combine lemon juice and honey and brush mixture onto cut side of pears. Preheat a grill pan or barbecue, then brush grill with oil. Grill pear halves, cut side down until golden and slightly softened, about 2–3 minutes. Remove from grill and serve warm with rice pudding.

Serves 8

GRILLED PEARS WITH WARM RICE PUDDING

Grilled mango and peaches with raspberry coulis

2 mangoes

4 peaches

2 tablespoons vegetable oil

FOR RASPBERRY COULIS

10 oz (300 g) fresh or frozen raspberries
  (thawed if frozen)

juice of 1 orange

2 tablespoons powdered (icing) sugar

Cut fleshy cheeks from mango and discard seed. Cut peaches in half and carefully remove seeds. Preheat a grill pan or barbecue, then brush grill with oil. Grill fruit until golden, about 1 minute each side. Remove from grill and serve warm or chilled with raspberry coulis.

To make raspberry coulis: Place raspberries, orange juice and sugar into a food processor and process until smooth. Refrigerate before serving.

Glossary

bean sprouts. Sprouting green mung beans are sold either fresh or canned, but the fresh tend to have more texture and flavor. Fresh sprouts can be stored in the refrigerator for 2–3 days.

bok choy. A small Asian variety of cabbage with thick white stems and mild-flavored dark green leaves, usually sold 3–4 in a bundle. If unavailable, use Chinese broccoli or choy sum.

cracked wheat. The whole wheat berry broken into coarse, medium or fine particles. Also called burghul.

cellophane noodles. Thin translucent dried noodles made from mung bean starch and sold in bundles. Also called bean thread noodles.

chili oil. Spicy oil produced by steeping dried red chili peppers in oil. Use this hot oil only by the drop. Store in refrigerator after opening.

choy sum. A Chinese green also known as flowering cabbage. It has yellow flowers, thin stems and a mild flavor and is suitable in most recipes that call for Chinese greens. The entire vegetable (stem, leaves and flowers) is used.

coconut cream and milk. The liquid extracted from grated coconut flesh after soaking in water. Coconut milk is thinner than coconut cream. Used extensively in Thai cooking, it is usually sold in cans.

curry pastes. A condiment consisting of curry seasonings and red or green chili peppers. The pastes are readily available in the supermarket, or you can make your own.

Red and green curry pastes are traditionally used in Thai cooking. Store in the refrigerator after opening.

hoisin sauce. Sweet, thick Chinese sauce, made from soybeans and also containing vinegar, sugar, chili peppers and other seasonings. Bottled hoisin sauce can be stored indefinitely in the refrigerator.

hot bean paste. A hot, thick red brown sauce made from fermented soybeans, chili peppers, garlic and spices. Sometimes called red bean paste or chili bean paste.

jasmine rice. Aromatic rice, popular in Thai cooking.

kaffir limes and lime leaves. Leaves from the kaffir lime tree are used to add an enticing citrus flavor and aroma to dishes. Dried leaves are readily available, but fresh ones can often be found. The juice and rind of the fruit are also used, but regular lime juice and rind can be substituted.

fish sauce. A pungent sauce of salted, fermented fish and other seasonings, used in sauces, dressings and dipping sauces. Products vary in intensity depending on the country of origin. Fish sauce from Thailand, called nam pla, is commonly available. Don't be put off by the strong fishy smell; there is really no substitute.

mirin. Sweet alcoholic wine made from rice and used in Japanese cooking. Sweet sherry can be substituted.

mizuna. A feathery Japanese salad green with a delicate flavor.

oyster sauce. A thick, dark brown Chinese sauce made from fermented dried oysters and soy sauce and sold in bottles. It is used to impart an intense or mildly briny flavor to stir-fries and other dishes. Store in refrigerator after opening.

palm sugar. Dense, heavy, dark cakes of sugar made from the sap of palms trees. Shave with a sharp knife or grate before using. Brown sugar can be used as a substitute. Available in Asian markets and many supermarkets.

rice wine. Sweet, low-alcohol Chinese wine, also known as shaoxing wine, made from glutinous rice. Sake or dry sherry can be used as a substitute.

sake. A clear Japanese wine made from fermented rice.

soy sauce. A salty sauce made from fermented soybeans and usually wheat, and sold in bottles and cans. Available in light and dark varieties, the dark is usually used in cooking and the lighter soy for dipping sauces.

sesame oil. An intensely flavored oil made from sesame seeds, sold in bottles, and widely used in Asian cooking. There is no real substitute.

shrimp paste. A pungent-flavored paste produced by drying, salting and pounding shrimp, then forming it into blocks or cakes.

tahini. A thick oily paste made from sesame seeds and traditionally used in Middle Eastern cooking.

Thai basil. Refers to several Asian basil varieties including holy, purple and sweet. Any basil can be used as a substitute.

Thai sweet chili sauce. A mild chili sauce with a sweet after taste. Usually used as a dipping sauce, it can also be used on burgers and barbecued meats. Store in refrigerator after opening.

wasabi paste. A traditional condiment served with Japanese sushi, made from a root similar to horseradish. Available as a paste or in powdered form to be mixed with water.

wonton wrappers. Thin sheets of wheat-based or egg-based dough, square or circular in shape, used to enclose a variety of fillings. Available fresh or frozen. Also called wonton skins or dumpling wrappers.

Index

Guide to weights and measures

The conversions given in the recipes in this book are approximate. Whichever system you use, remember to follow it consistently, thereby ensuring that the proportions are consistent throughout a recipe.

WEIGHTS

Imperial	Metric
⅓ oz	10 g
½ oz	15 g
¾ oz	20 g
1 oz	30 g
2 oz	60 g
3 oz	90 g
4 oz (¼ lb)	125 g
5 oz (⅓ lb)	150 g
6 oz	180 g
7 oz	220 g
8 oz (½ lb)	250 g
9 oz	280 g
10 oz	300 g
11 oz	330 g
12 oz (¾ lb)	375 g
16 oz (1 lb)	500 g
2 lb	1 kg
3 lb	1.5 kg
4 lb	2 kg

USEFUL CONVERSIONS

¼ teaspoon	1.25 ml
½ teaspoon	2.5 ml
1 teaspoon	5 ml
1 Australian tablespoon	20 ml (4 teaspoons)
1 UK/US tablespoon	15 ml (3 teaspoons)

Butter/Shortening

1 tablespoon	½ oz	15 g
1½ tablespoons	¾ oz	20 g
2 tablespoons	1 oz	30 g
3 tablespoons	1½ oz	45 g

OVEN TEMPERATURE GUIDE

The Celsius (°C) and Fahrenheit (°F) temperatures in this chart apply to most electric ovens. Decrease by 25°F or 10°C for a gas oven or refer to the manufacturer's temperature guide. For temperatures below 325°F (160°C), do not decrease the given temperature.

VOLUME

Imperial	Metric	Cup
1 fl oz	30 ml	
2 fl oz	60 ml	¼
3 fl oz	90 ml	⅓
4 fl oz	125 ml	½
5 fl oz	150 ml	⅔
6 fl oz	180 ml	¾
8 fl oz	250 ml	1
10 fl oz	300 ml	1¼
12 fl oz	375 ml	1½
13 fl oz	400 ml	1⅔
14 fl oz	440 ml	1¾
16 fl oz	500 ml	2
24 fl oz	750 ml	3
32 fl oz	1L	4

Oven description	°C	°F	Gas Mark
Cool	110	225	¼
	130	250	½
Very slow	140	275	1
	150	300	2
Slow	170	325	3
Moderate	180	350	4
	190	375	5
Moderately Hot	200	400	6
Fairly Hot	220	425	7
Hot	230	450	8
Very Hot	240	475	9
Extremely Hot	250	500	10

First published in the United States in 2001 by Periplus Editions (HK) Ltd.,
with editorial offices at 153 Milk Street, Boston, Massachusetts 02109 and
130 Joo Seng Road, #06-01/03, Singapore 368357

ISBN 962-593-937-7

DISTRIBUTED BY

North America, Latin America
(*English Language*)
Tuttle Publishing
364 Innovation Drive
North Clarendon, VT 05759-9436
Tel: (802) 773-8930 Fax: (802) 773-6993
Email: info@tuttlepublishing.com
www.tuttlepublishing.com

Japan
Tuttle Publishing
Yaekari Building, 3rd Floor
5-4-12 Osaki, Shinagawa-ku
Tokyo 141-0032
Tel: (03) 5437-0171 Fax: (03) 5437-0755
Email: tuttle-sales@gol.com

Asia Pacific
Berkeley Books Pte Ltd
130 Joo Seng Road #06-01/03, Singapore 368357
Tel: (65) 6280 1330 Fax: (65) 6280 6290
Email: inquiries@periplus.com.sg
www.periplus.com

Set in Frutiger on QuarkXPress
Printed in Singapore

First Edition
05 06 07 08 09 8 7 6 5 4 3 2